RHODES GREECE TRAVEL GUIDE 2023

Unraveling the Legends of Rhodes: Your Captivating Travel Guide to Greece's Timeless Island of Knights

D1216505

Donald M. Clark

Table of content

Introduction

Welcome to Rhodes, a beautiful island situated in the crystal-clear seas of the Aegean Sea. With a rich tapestry of history, lively culture, and spectacular natural beauty, Rhodes has captured the hearts of tourists for centuries. As you begin on your adventure to this unique Greek island, allow us to be your guide and unveil the mysteries that lie behind its historic walls and sun-kissed coastlines.

Rhodes, the biggest of the Dodecanese islands, features a fascinating history that resonates through its cobblestone alleys, ancient ruins, and medieval architecture. From the mythological legends of the Colossus of Rhodes to the grandeur of the

Palace of the Grand Master, this island is a living witness to the civilizations that have influenced its fate.

Beyond its historical treasures, Rhodes greets tourists with its warm Mediterranean friendliness. The island is famed for its gorgeous beaches, where turquoise seas softly lap golden dunes, encouraging you to relax and enjoy the island's everlasting sunlight. Explore secret coves, participate in daring water sports experiences, or just relax on a peaceful day beneath a parasol, appreciating the excellent food and cool beverages that await you.

For the intrepid tourist, Rhodes offers a multitude of adventures outside its boundaries. Discover quaint communities buried away in the island's interior, where time appears to stand still. Immerse yourself in local customs, witness enthralling festivals, and experience the delights of real Greek food in family-run tavernas.

Throughout this travel guide, we will steer you through the must-see sights, off-the-beaten-path jewels, and insider recommendations that will make your vacation to Rhodes memorable. Whether you're seeking history, adventure, leisure, or a combination of it all, Rhodes has something unique in store for you.

So, begin on this voyage with an open heart and an excited spirit. Let Rhodes bewitch you with its ancient appeal, captivate you with its natural beauties, and leave an unforgettable impact on your spirit. The voyage starts, and Rhodes awaits to impart its ageless enchantment.

20 Reasons Why I Love Rhodes And Why You Should Visit

Rhodes, the Island of the Knights, is a compelling place that has captivated the hearts of countless tourists, including mine. With its rich history, spectacular natural beauty, kind hospitality, and lively culture, Rhodes provides a fantastic experience for travelers. In this guide, I will give my reasons why I adore Rhodes and why you should consider visiting this beautiful island.

1. Historical Significance:

Rhodes is a rich mine of history, reaching back to ancient times. The island was previously home to the Colossus of Rhodes, one of the Seven Wonders of the Ancient World. Exploring the Rhodes Old Town, a

UNESCO World Heritage site, is like going back in time. The medieval fortifications, the Palace of the Grand Master, and the Street of the Knights are awe-inspiring and give a sense of the island's historic history.

2. Rhodes Old Town:

One of the primary reasons I adore Rhodes is its lovely Old Town. It is the biggest inhabited medieval town in Europe and is filled with charm. The narrow cobblestone lanes, the colorful houses, and the medieval architecture create a beautiful ambiance. Getting lost in the maze-like alleyways, stumbling across secret squares, and finding tiny stores and old tavernas is a treat.

3. Magnificent Beaches:

Rhodes is endowed with some of the most magnificent beaches in the Mediterranean. From immaculate sandy coasts to quiet coves, there is a beach for everyone. I especially enjoy Tsambika Beach, with its crystal-clear blue waves and golden beach. The beach in Lindos, with the Acropolis as its background, is another favorite of mine. Whether you prefer leisure, sea sports, or bustling beach bars, Rhodes offers it all.

4. Rich Cultural Heritage:

The cultural heritage of Rhodes is intriguing. The island has been affected by different civilizations throughout history, including the Greeks, Romans, Byzantines, Knights of Saint John, and Ottomans. This rich background is evident in the architecture, food, and customs. Exploring the ancient sites, visiting museums, and experiencing traditional festivals and events let you immerse yourself in this rich cultural tapestry.

5. Warm Hospitality:

Greek hospitality is famous, and Rhodes is no exception. The residents are polite, friendly, and proud of their island. From the time you arrive, you'll be welcomed with warm grins and genuine friendliness. Interacting with the people and witnessing their way of life adds an added element of authenticity to your stay.

6. Delicious Cuisine:

Greek cuisine is a joy for food connoisseurs, and Rhodes delivers a delightful gastronomic experience. From fresh seafood to scrumptious souvlaki, traditional mezes (small plates) to sweet pleasures like loukoumades, your taste buds will be in for a treat. I strongly suggest tasting local delicacies like "saganaki" (fried cheese), "moussaka" (layered meal with eggplant and meat), and "gyro" (grilled beef in pita bread).

7. Natural Beauty and Landscapes:

Rhodes has different landscapes and natural beauty. From the lush green valleys of Petaloudes (Valley of the Butterflies) to the craggy mountains of Profitis Ilias, the island provides spectacular sights at every turn. Exploring the charming towns of Lindos, Archangelos, and Embona enables you to experience traditional Greek island life among stunning surroundings.

8. Island Hopping Opportunities:

Rhodes provides a good location for island hopping in the Dodecanese archipelago. You may easily embark on day vacations or short visits to surrounding islands including Symi, Kos, and Patmos. Each island has its particular beauty and attractions, allowing a chance to widen your exploration and discover more of the Greek island paradise.

9. Vibrant Nightlife:

Rhodes is recognized for its active nightlife, notably in Faliraki and Rhodes Town. Whether you like boisterous beach bars, elegant clubs, or quaint tavernas with live music, there is a location to suit every taste. The atmosphere is electrifying, and the island comes alive after sunset, giving amazing evenings of entertainment and pleasure.

10. Accessibility and Infrastructure:

Rhodes is well-connected and readily accessible, making it a handy destination for vacationers. The island has an international airport with direct flights from many European cities. Ferry links from Athens and other Greek islands are also available. The tourist infrastructure on the island is well-developed, enabling a pleasant and pleasurable visit.

11. Outdoor Activities and Adventure:

Rhodes is a haven for outdoor lovers and adventure seekers. The island provides a broad choice of activities to get your adrenaline racing. From hiking and trekking through gorgeous paths in the highlands to cycling along seaside roads, there are lots of possibilities to discover Rhodes' natural surroundings. Water activities such as snorkeling, scuba diving, windsurfing, and sailing are other popular alternatives for individuals seeking aquatic experiences.

12. Festivals and Celebrations:

Rhodes is noted for its vivid festivals and festivities, which give a unique view into the island's cultural past. The Medieval Rose Festival, held yearly in Rhodes Town, transports tourists back in time with medieval reenactments, parades, and traditional music and dance performances. Other events, like the Wine Festival in Embona and the Panagia Tsambika Festival, allow exploring local customs, eating regional foods, and enjoying exciting celebrations.

13. Shopping and Souvenirs:

Rhodes provides a wonderful shopping experience, merging contemporary stores with historic markets and artisan shops. In Rhodes Town, you'll discover a mix of worldwide brands, fashionable stores, and local crafts. The Mandraki Harbor area is perfect for souvenir shopping, with a variety of stores providing traditional items including pottery, olive oil, spices, and handcrafted jewelry. Exploring the local markets, such as the Agora Market, enables you to immerse yourself in the island's colorful environment and locate unique souvenirs to take home.

14. Wellness and Relaxation:

Rhodes is not only about history and adventure; it also provides opportunities for leisure and renewal. The island is home to several health retreats, spa resorts, and wellness facilities where you may indulge in treatments, yoga sessions, and holistic therapies. Enjoy a day of pampering, rest on the calm beaches, and appreciate the serene ambiance that Rhodes provides.

15. Family-Friendly Destination:

Rhodes is a fantastic location for families since it caters to a broad variety of interests and ages. From child-friendly beaches with shallow seas to water parks and entertainment centers, there are lots of things to keep the young ones amused. Exploring the historic alleyways, visiting the Rhodes Aquarium, and enjoying a boat excursion along the coastline are just a few examples of family-friendly adventures the island has to offer.

16. Sunsets and Scenic Views:

Witnessing a Rhodes sunset is a magnificent experience. Whether you're having a romantic supper overlooking the Aegean Sea or catching the sun's last rays from a high vantage point, the island provides spectacular panoramic views that will leave you in amazement. The mix of golden colors, the shimmering water, and the shadows of ancient ruins create a spectacular sight.

17. Cultural Events and Performances:

Rhodes holds different cultural events and performances throughout the year, showing its artistic and creative side. From open-air concerts and theatrical shows to art exhibits and traditional music performances, there's always something to enjoy. Keep an eye out for events like the Rhodes International Film Festival and the Rhodes Rock Festival to immerse yourself in the island's cultural landscape.

18. Warm Mediterranean Climate:

Rhodes benefits from a lovely Mediterranean environment, characterized by moderate winters and long, sunny summers. The island boasts around 300 days of sunlight every year, making it a great location for visitors seeking warmth and Vitamin D. The Mediterranean climate allows for year-round vacations, with each season presenting its distinct appeal and activities.

19. Romantic Getaway:

With its beautiful ancient town, breathtaking sunsets, and scenic environs, Rhodes is a fantastic place for couples seeking a romantic break. Stroll hand in hand through the small alleyways of the Old Town, have a candlelight meal overlooking the sea, or take a leisurely boat journey to the adjacent island of Symi for a romantic day excursion. Rhodes sets the setting for wonderful moments with your loved one.

20. Authentic Greek Experience:

Rhodes provides a genuine Greek experience, enabling you to immerse yourself in the native way of life. From sampling traditional Greek food to participating in cultural rituals and festivals, you'll have the chance to interact with the island's rich legacy. The warm welcome, real encounters with people, and the island's bustling ambiance all add to a genuinely authentic Greek experience.

In conclusion, Rhodes is a mesmerizing site that provides a plethora of reasons to come. Its rich history, gorgeous scenery, kind hospitality, and lively culture make it a remarkable experience for tourists. Whether you're seeking adventure, leisure, cultural immersion, or a romantic retreat, Rhodes has something to offer everyone. Embark on a voyage to this magical island and uncover the riches that await you.

20 Top-Rated Tourist Attractions In Rhodes

Rhodes, the magnificent island of the Knights, is a place that catches the hearts of tourists with its rich history, breathtaking beaches, and dynamic culture. If you're planning a vacation to Rhodes, here are some of the top-rated tourist sites that you might consider adding to your schedule. Each site provides a distinct experience and an insight into the island's intriguing past.

1. Rhodes Old Town:

Rhodes Old Town, a UNESCO World Heritage site, is a must-visit sight. Enclosed behind ancient walls, the Old Town is the oldest inhabited medieval town in Europe. It is a maze of little alleyways, dramatic squares, and spectacular monuments. The Street of the Knights, flanked by the homes of the Knights of Saint John, is a notable landmark. The Palace of the Grand Master, a reconstructed medieval fortress, is another prominent building that shouldn't be missed. Exploring the Old Town is like going back in time and immersing yourself in the island's intriguing history.

2. Lindos Acropolis:

Perched on a hill overlooking the Aegean Sea, the Lindos Acropolis is a fascinating archaeological monument. This old fortress shows the ruins of many civilizations, including the Greeks, Romans, Byzantines, and Knights of Saint John. The Acropolis is capped by the Temple of Athena Lindia, affording stunning panoramic views of the surrounding coastline. As you mount the hill, you'll pass through the lovely hamlet of Lindos, noted for its whitewashed buildings and small lanes.

3. Valley of the Butterflies (Petaloudes):

Nature aficionados will be charmed by the lovely Valley of the Butterflies. Located near the town of Petaloudes, this fascinating natural reserve is home to hundreds of multicolored butterflies. During the summer months, the valley comes alive as the Jersey Tiger Moths cover the trees and create a stunning display. Walking along the authorized walkways, surrounded by lush foliage and the soft flapping of wings, is a tranquil and lovely experience.

4. Prasonisi:

For windsurfing and kiteboarding lovers, Prasonisi is heaven. Located at the southernmost extremity of Rhodes, Prasonisi is a peninsula that provides great conditions for water activities. With powerful winds and a unique configuration where the Aegean Sea meets the Mediterranean, it offers a playground for thrill-seekers. Even if you're not into water sports, viewing the bright sails and stunning stunts done by competitors is a captivating sight.

5. Ancient Kamiros:

Step back in time to the ancient city of Kamiros. Once one of the island's most powerful towns, Kamiros is now an archaeological site that exhibits the ruins of a well-planned Hellenistic-Roman metropolis. As you tour the site, you may meander through the old streets, see the public buildings, and enjoy the surviving mosaics and the remnants of private residences. The site gives a fascinating view into the everyday lives of the ancient people of Rhodes.

6. Rhodes Aquarium:

The Rhodes Aquarium, situated in the northern portion of the island, is an educational and entertaining attraction. It holds a vast diversity of marine life, including colorful fish, sea turtles, and uncommon species found in the Mediterranean Sea. The aquarium strives to promote awareness about the significance of marine conservation and gives visitors a chance to watch and learn about these amazing species up close.

7. Tsambika Monastery and Beach:

Perched on a hill overlooking the eastern shore of Rhodes, Tsambika Monastery is a prominent religious landmark on the island. According to tradition, it is thought that women who are suffering to conceive might seek the graces of the Virgin Mary at the convent. The panoramic views from the summit are spectacular. After touring the monastery, you may travel down to Tsambika Beach, a magnificent length of beach and turquoise seas, where you can relax and soak up the sun.

8. Rhodes Town Beaches:

Rhodes is famed for its magnificent beaches, and Rhodes Town itself provides various alternatives for beach enthusiasts. Elli Beach, situated in the middle of the city, is a popular option with its golden beaches, clean seas, and active environment. It provides a variety of attractions, including beach bars, water sports, and sunbed rentals. Other beaches around Rhodes Town include Akti Miaouli and Zephyros Beach, giving calm locations to rest and enjoy the coastline scenery.

9. Filerimos Monastery and Hill:

Filerimos Monastery, situated on Filerimos Hill, is a tranquil retreat and a center of historical and theological importance. The monastery goes back to the Byzantine period and has exquisite murals and icons. As you mount the hill, you'll face the stunning 18-meter-tall cross, affording panoramic views of the surrounding area. The scenic promenade, bordered by cypress trees, contributes to the serene mood of the place.

10. Seven Springs (Epta Pages):

Escape to the beautiful paradise of Seven Springs, a hidden treasure buried away in the hills of Rhodes. As the name implies, Seven Springs is distinguished by crystal-clear water that runs from natural springs, providing a quiet and relaxing setting. You may wander along the shaded paths, cross the wooden bridge across the creek, and have a picnic in the serene natural surroundings. Don't miss the opportunity to explore the dark tunnel, which leads to a tiny lake and adds a bit of mystique to the experience.

11. Monolithos Castle:

Perched on a rocky mountaintop, Monolithos Castle looks into Rhodes' medieval history and breathtaking panoramic vistas. The fortress, dating back to the 15th century, was erected by the Knights of Saint John to safeguard the island from attackers. Although only ruins remain, the walk to the summit is rewarded with stunning panoramas of the surrounding mountains and the Aegean Sea.

12. Kallithea Springs:

Kallithea Springs is a historical complex that was formerly a prominent spa resort. The beautiful building, boasting a combination of Oriental and Art Deco forms, offers a distinctive and exquisite ambiance. Today, the complex has been rebuilt and serves as a location for gatherings, weddings, and cultural displays. The quiet gardens, exquisite mosaics, and the option to take a bath in the revitalizing thermal waters make Kallithea Springs a popular destination.

13. Haraki:

Escape the throng and visit the lovely town of Haraki, tucked on the eastern coast of Rhodes. Haraki provides a laid-back environment and a gorgeous beach, suitable for visitors wanting a relaxed day by the sea. The pebble beach is dotted with traditional tavernas selling fresh seafood, and the tranquil seas are great for swimming and snorkeling. It's a hidden treasure where you may enjoy the real charm of a classic Greek fishing hamlet.

14. The Street of the Knights:

The thoroughfare of the Knights, situated inside the Rhodes Old Town, is a beautiful thoroughfare that symbolizes the island's medieval origins. It was previously the seat of the Knights of Saint John and is bordered by magnificently preserved medieval structures, each representing a distinct linguistic group. Walking along this ancient street helps you to picture the majesty of the knights' period and admire the architectural brilliance of the time.

15. Embona Village:

Venture into the heart of Rhodes and explore the traditional hamlet of Embona. Nestled between vineyards and mountains, Embona gives a peek into rural Greek life. The hamlet is famed for its wine production, and you may visit neighboring vineyards to enjoy the renowned Rhodian wines. Explore the picturesque alleys, explore the small stores offering handcrafted handicrafts, and eat real Greek food in the traditional tavernas.

16. Ancient Stadium of Rhodes:

The Ancient Stadium of Rhodes, situated near the Temple of Apollo, is an amazing archaeological monument. Dating back to the 3rd century BC, it was formerly a location for athletic tournaments and is thought to have housed up to 30,000 people. The site gives an insight into the athletic culture of ancient Rhodes and the splendor of the stadium.

17. Profitis Ilias Mountain:

For spectacular panoramic views of Rhodes, a visit to Profitis Ilias Mountain is a necessity. Located in the center of the island, the mountain is the tallest point in Rhodes and provides beautiful panoramas of the surrounding surroundings. You may drive or trek to the peak, where you'll discover a modest church dedicated to Profitis Ilias (Prophet Elijah). On a good day, you may even see as far as the neighboring islands.

18. Archaeological Museum of Rhodes:

Immerse yourself in Rhodes' rich history and historical riches at the Historical Museum of Rhodes. The museum exhibits a magnificent collection of items, including sculptures, ceramics, jewelry, and mosaics, going back to prehistoric times. It gives insight into the island's numerous historical eras and civilizations, enabling visitors to dive further into its cultural history.

19. Anthony Quinn Bay:

Named after the legendary actor who fell in love with Rhodes while shooting "The Guns of Navarone," Anthony Quinn Bay is a lovely cove noted for its crystal-clear turquoise seas and gorgeous natural surroundings. The bay provides an excellent location for swimming and snorkeling, with an underwater world filled with marine life. Sunbathing on the rocky platforms and enjoying the calm of the bay is a fantastic way to relax.

20. Symi Island:

Although technically not part of Rhodes, a day excursion to Symi Island is highly recommended. Located only a short boat trip away, Symi is a tiny island highlighted by colorful neoclassical residences and a picturesque port. Explore the small alleyways, see the majestic Monastery of Panormitis, and appreciate the quiet ambiance of this gorgeous island.

These top-rated tourist sites in Rhodes provide a varied variety of experiences, enabling you to immerse yourself in the island's history, natural beauty, and cultural legacy. Whether you're a history enthusiast, a nature lover, or just seeking leisure,

Rhodes offers something to enchant every tourist. Embark on a visit to this wonderful island and make memories that will last a lifetime.

Rhodes Travel Cost and Tourists Visa

Rhodes, the picturesque Greek island in the Aegean Sea, provides a mesmerizing combination of history, natural beauty, and dynamic culture. To plan your trip successfully and spend sensibly, it is vital to understand the travel expenses and visa requirements for visiting Rhodes. This book gives thorough information on travel expenditures and tourist permits, letting you plan your Rhodes journey with confidence.

Travel Costs

1. Accommodation:

Accommodation expenses in Rhodes vary based on the season, location, and kind of stay. Options vary from budget-friendly hostels and guesthouses to mid-range hotels and luxury resorts. Prices tend to be higher in prominent tourist places such as Rhodes Town or Lindos. Consider staying in less popular regions or reserving in advance to receive cheaper discounts. On average, budget-conscious tourists may expect to pay roughly €20-50 per night for affordable hotels.

2. Food and Dining:

Rhodes provides several eating alternatives to suit various budgets. Traditional tavernas and small diners provide economical Greek food, while foreign restaurants and sophisticated places may be costly. To save money, go for street food or local markets where you can get fresh fruit, bread, and snacks for budget-friendly meals. On average, budget travelers may expect to spend roughly €10-20 per day on meals.

3. Transportation:

Getting to Rhodes is reasonably inexpensive, with various transportation alternatives available. Public buses are a cost-effective method to commute between cities and villages, with costs beginning at roughly €2. Taxis are more costly yet useful for shorter trips or group transport. Renting a vehicle or scooter gives freedom but increases gasoline and rental fees. Budget for an average of €20-30 each day on transportation, depending on your chosen method of travel.

4. Sightseeing and Activities:

Rhodes is rich in historical landmarks, cultural attractions, and natural beauty. While many sights have entry prices, they are often reasonable. The admission costs for major monuments like the Rhodes Old Town or the Acropolis of Lindos vary from €6-12. Some sites offer reduced or combination tickets, so plan your schedule appropriately. Additionally, allow for additional fees such as guided tours, boat cruises, or water sports if you choose to partake in these activities.

5. Miscellaneous Expenses:

Allocate a percentage of your budget for incidental expenditures such as souvenirs, shopping, and unplanned fees. Rhodes provides a range of stores, marketplaces, and boutiques where you may discover unique gifts or local items. Keep in mind that negotiating is prevalent in marketplaces, helping you to achieve better discounts. It's also important to maintain a contingency fund for emergencies, unforeseen transportation changes, or medical bills.

Tourist Visa

1. Visa Requirements:

Greece, including Rhodes, is a part of the Schengen Area, which means that people from numerous countries may visit without a visa for short-term tourists. However, it's vital to examine the individual visa requirements depending on your nationality. Citizens of the European Union (EU) and the European Free Trade Association (EFTA) nations may enter with a valid passport or national ID card. Non-EU nationals may need a Schengen Visa, which enables stays of up to 90 days within 180 days.

2. Visa Application Process:

If you need a Schengen Visa, the application procedure normally comprises obtaining the requisite papers, filling out the application form, and booking an appointment at the right consulate or embassy. The needed papers may include a valid passport, evidence of lodging, travel itinerary, travel insurance, proof of financial means, and a completed application form. It's necessary to apply well in advance to allow for processing time.

3. Duration of Stay:

With a tourist visa, you may remain in Rhodes for up to 90 days within 180 days. It's crucial to stick to the visa restrictions and not overstay your allotted time. If you want to remain longer or have other goals, such as studying or working, other visa requirements may apply, and it's required to check the appropriate Greek consular services or embassy.

4. Travel Insurance:

While not a visa requirement, obtaining travel insurance is strongly advised while visiting Rhodes or any overseas country. Travel insurance offers coverage for medical emergencies, travel cancellations or interruptions, lost luggage, and other unanticipated occurrences. Ensure that your insurance policy contains appropriate coverage for your activities and length of stay in Rhodes.

In Conclusion, Understanding the travel expenses and visa requirements for Rhodes is vital for organizing a successful and budget-friendly vacation. By accounting for housing, meals, transportation, sightseeing, and incidental expenditures, you may construct a realistic budget that meets your trip style. Additionally, researching and meeting the appropriate visa procedures will assure a hassle-free arrival to Rhodes. With appropriate planning, you may fully enjoy the beauty and culture of Rhodes while controlling your spending and complying with visa rules.

Backpacking Rhodes Recommended Budgets

Backpacking in Rhodes provides a unique and budget-friendly way to explore this intriguing Greek island. With its rich history, magnificent beaches, and lively culture, Rhodes is a perfect location for travelers wanting an exciting and immersive experience. This book gives suggested budgets and practical advice to help you plan your hiking trip to Rhodes without breaking the bank.

1. Accommodation Budget:

When it comes to housing, backpackers have various budget-friendly choices to pick from. Hostels and guesthouses are popular alternatives, providing economical dormitory-style or private rooms. Prices vary based on location and amenities, so consider staying beyond the major tourist regions for more budget-friendly choices. Another alternative is camping since Rhodes offers various campgrounds that give basic facilities at a lesser cost.

2. Food and Dining Budget:

To keep your meal spending in control, discover local cafés and tavernas that serve traditional Greek cuisine at moderate pricing. Opt for street cuisine like souvlaki or gyros, which are satisfying and inexpensive. Visit local markets to acquire fresh fruit, bread, and snacks for budget-friendly dinners. Additionally, make use of self-catering facilities if your property permits cooking, since making your meals may drastically reduce expenditures.

3. Transportation Budget:

Public transportation, like buses, is the most budget-friendly method for moving about Rhodes. Purchase a multi-day bus ticket, which permits unlimited travel and delivers exceptional value for money. Plan your route in a manner that avoids the need for taxis or rental automobiles, since these may rapidly eat into your budget. Embrace walking and cycling wherever feasible, since Rhodes provides breathtaking landscapes and picturesque routes that are best experienced on foot or by bike.

4. Sightseeing and Activities Budget:

Rhodes provides a multitude of sights and activities that won't stretch your wallet. Many historical places, including the Rhodes Old Town, offer free or low-cost admission fees, enabling you to discover the island's rich legacy without breaking the bank. Take advantage of free walking tours or self-guided excursions to learn about the island's history and culture. Enjoy the island's natural beauty by spending time on its public beaches, hiking gorgeous paths, or just walking through lovely towns.

5. Nightlife and Entertainment Budget:

Rhodes has a busy nightlife scene, notably in tourist districts like Rhodes Town and Faliraki. While certain clubs and pubs might be costly, there are budget-friendly choices accessible. Look for happy hour offers and drink specials, or pick small tavernas and taverns that provide live music and entertainment without charging expensive cover fees. Take part in cultural events or festivals, which typically include traditional music and dance performances, delivering a memorable experience at little or no expense.

6. Shopping and Souvenirs Budget:

Set a particular budget for shopping and souvenirs to prevent overpaying. While it's tempting to bring back keepsakes from your vacation, be careful and concentrate on things that carry personal importance. Visit local markets or smaller stores where you may frequently discover interesting and cheaply priced goods. Remember to barter and negotiate pricing, since this may occasionally result in large discounts, especially in marketplaces or smaller venues.

7. Emergency Fund:

Set aside a percentage of your budget as an emergency fund to allow for unforeseen expenditures or events that may happen during your backpacking vacation. This money may be used for unanticipated transportation expenditures, medical crises, or last-minute accommodation adjustments. Having an emergency fund gives peace of mind and saves any financial hardship if unforeseen circumstances arise.

8. Prioritize Free and Low-Cost Activities:

Rhodes provides several free or low-cost activities that give a diverse and genuine experience. Take advantage of public beaches, coastal treks, and touring picturesque towns without any admission fees. Attend local festivals or cultural events, which frequently give free or low admittance and display the island's customs and history. By prioritizing these activities, you may have a great backpacking vacation without sacrificing your money.

In Conclusion, Backpacking in Rhodes may be a budget-friendly vacation, enabling you to see the island's beauty, history, and culture without breaking the bank. By carefully controlling your lodging, food, transportation, sightseeing, and entertainment expenditures, you can create a wonderful backpacking vacation that meets your budget. Remember to put experiences above material belongings and enjoy the simplicity of backpacking while immersing yourself in the particular charm of Rhodes.

Rhodes Money Saving Tips

Rhodes, the picturesque Greek island in the Aegean Sea, provides a plethora of activities, from ancient ruins to breathtaking beaches. To make your vacation more economical without sacrificing enjoyment, using money-saving methods is crucial. This book offers you practical suggestions and information to help you save money while touring Rhodes.

1. Travel During the Off-Season:

Consider visiting Rhodes during the shoulder or off-peak seasons, often from April to June and September to October. During these periods, lodging and airfares are frequently more reasonable, and major sights are less crowded. You may take advantage of lesser pricing while still enjoying good weather and a more relaxed attitude.

2. Plan and Book in Advance:

Take the time to organize your vacation well in advance, including lodging, airfare, and activities. By booking early, you may typically score better offers and discounts. Look for package offers that combine flights and hotels or take advantage of early bird bargains. Research several booking sites and compare costs to locate the cheapest bargains.

3. Stay in Self-Catering Accommodation:

Consider staying in self-catering accommodations such as flats or villas that come with a kitchenette or complete kitchen. This enables you to make your meals instead of dining out for every meal. Visit local markets or supermarkets to buy fresh vegetables and goods, which may be more budget-friendly than eating at restaurants for every meal.

4. Explore Local Cuisine:

While eating out is a lovely part of any trip experience, go for local cafés and tavernas that serve traditional Greek food at more inexpensive costs compared to tourist-oriented places. Sample classic foods such as souvlaki, moussaka, and Greek salads. Ask locals for tips to find hidden treasures that serve wonderful meals at cheap costs.

5. Take Advantage of Free Activities:

Rhodes boasts numerous free or low-cost activities that enable you to see the island without breaking the budget. Explore the ancient Old Town, enjoy public beaches, and meander through local markets. Attend cultural festivals and gatherings, which generally exhibit traditional music, dance, and performances. Enjoy walks along picturesque coastline trails and enjoy the island's natural beauty without paying a thing.

6. Utilize Public Transportation:

Public transportation, like buses, is a cost-effective method to move about Rhodes. The island has a comprehensive transportation network that links major cities and attractions. Purchase a daily or weekly bus pass, which enables unlimited travel and may save you money compared to individual tickets. Plan your route to maximize your usage of public transit and eliminate the need for taxis or rental automobiles.

7. Embrace Walking and Cycling:

Rhodes provides stunning scenery and lovely cities that may be visited on foot or by bicycle. Walking is a terrific method to explore secret nooks, historical landmarks, and local communities. Rent a bicycle to explore coastal trails and picturesque roads. Not only will you save money on commuting, but you'll also have a more immersive and ecologically responsible experience.

8. Visit Free or Discounted Attractions:

Research attractions that give free admission or cheap access on specified days or at certain periods. For example, certain museums and historical sites in Rhodes provide free entry on particular days of the week. Take advantage of these possibilities to experience the island's cultural and historical treasures without paying extra expenditures.

9. Pack Smart and Travel Light:

Avoid extra baggage costs by packing light and conforming to your airline's luggage rules. Pack adaptable attire appropriate for diverse weather conditions and activities. Bring reusable water bottles to replenish at public fountains or your hotel to avoid buying bottled water, which may rapidly add up.

10. Bargain and Negotiate:

In local markets and smaller businesses, don't be scared to barter and negotiate pricing. While it may not be relevant in bigger businesses or fixed-price shops, bargaining may occasionally result in receiving a better rate, particularly for souvenirs or local items. Be courteous and considerate while bargaining, and remember that it's part of the cultural experience in certain areas.

In Conclusion, By applying these money-saving ideas, you may have a budget-friendly vacation to Rhodes without sacrificing the quality of your experience. Remember to prepare ahead, be cautious of your spending, and explore local culture and food. With careful planning and a little ingenuity, you can make lasting memories on this lovely Greek island while keeping your travel expenditures under control.

How to Travel Around Rhodes

Rhodes, the lovely Greek island in the Dodecanese, provides a broad selection of activities, from ancient ruins and medieval villages to beautiful beaches and breathtaking landscapes. To truly appreciate the island's charms, it is vital to know the numerous transportation alternatives accessible. This thorough guide will offer you crucial information on how to navigate Rhodes, including forms of transportation, advice for getting around, and suggested routes.

1. Renting a Car:

Renting a vehicle is one of the most convenient ways to explore Rhodes, allowing flexibility and the ability to uncover hidden treasures at your leisure. Major automobile rental firms operate on the island, offering a broad selection of cars to meet your requirements. It is important to reserve in advance, particularly during high seasons, and ensure you have a valid driver's license. Familiarize oneself with local driving rules and restrictions before hitting the road.

2. Public Buses:

Rhodes has a well-developed public bus network that links major cities and famous tourist attractions. The buses are pleasant, air-conditioned, and moderately priced. Rhodes Town serves as the core center, with routes spreading to other sections of the island. Timetables and route maps are available at bus stops or online. Plan your route, including transport timings and connections.

3. Taxis:

Taxis are frequently accessible in Rhodes, especially in tourist areas and near transit hubs. Official taxis are identified by their characteristic yellow hue and LED roof signs. It is recommended to urge that the driver turns on the taximeter at the beginning of the journey to guarantee a fair fee. Taxis may also be rented for longer periods or bespoke trips, but negotiate the fee in advance.

4. Scooter or Motorcycle Rental:

For shorter trips and touring smaller towns and villages, renting a scooter or motorbike may be a fun and handy alternative. Many rental firms provide scooters and motorbikes for hiring, and they are especially popular among younger visitors. Ensure you have a valid driver's license for two-wheeled vehicles and wear adequate safety gear, including helmets.

5. Bicycle Rental:

Rhodes features gorgeous scenery and lovely coastline paths, making cycling a terrific way to explore the island. Several rental firms provide bicycles, including mountain bikes and electric bikes, catering to varied interests and fitness levels. Consider renting a bicycle for a day or joining a guided riding trip to explore secret routes and stunning landscapes.

6. Ferries & Boat Tours:

Rhodes is well-connected to neighboring islands and mainland Greece by ferry services. Ferries run from Rhodes Town and nearby ports, giving opportunity for island hopping and day vacations. Explore the adjacent islands of Symi, and Kos, or perhaps go farther to Crete. Additionally, boat cruises and excursions are provided, presenting new viewpoints of Rhodes' coastline, isolated beaches, and adjacent islands.

7. Walking and Exploring on Foot:

Rhodes Town, with its attractive historic Old Town, is best explored on foot. Wander through its small cobblestone alleyways, see ancient ruins, and visit historic sites. Walking enables you to thoroughly immerse yourself in the environment and unearth hidden jewels that may not be accessible by other forms of transportation. Pack comfortable shoes, and a map, and begin on a self-guided walking tour.

8. Guided Tours & Excursions:

To make the most of your stay in Rhodes and obtain in-depth information about the island's history and culture, consider taking guided tours and excursions. Local tour providers offer a broad choice of alternatives, including historical excursions, cultural experiences, hiking treks, and gastronomic adventures. These trips feature skilled guides who can give useful insights and assure a well-organized itinerary.

9. Navigating Rhodes Town:

Rhodes Town may be explored on foot or by utilizing the local transit alternatives indicated above. The town is separated into two major areas: the historic Old Town and the contemporary New Town. The Old Town is a UNESCO World Heritage Site and is best visited on foot owing to its small alleys and ancient attractions. The New Town features broader boulevards and provides a dynamic environment with stores, restaurants, and nightlife.

10. Planning Your Routes:

To maximize your time and guarantee a seamless travel experience, plan your routes. Consider the sights and places you desire to see, taking into mind their proximity and the most efficient way of transportation. Create an itinerary that gives you appropriate time at each place while factoring in transit schedules and any delays.

In Conclusion, Traveling to Rhodes is a fascinating trip, enabling you to see the island's natural beauty, historical riches, and lovely communities. By using the many kinds of transportation available, planning your routes properly, and being open to new experiences, you can create an exciting voyage full of adventure and discovery. Enjoy the different scenery, enjoy the local culture, and cherish every minute as you travel to the wonderful island of Rhodes.

How To Be Safe In Rhodes

Rhodes, the lovely Greek island in the Dodecanese, provides a combination of history, natural beauty, and dynamic culture. While it is typically a safe site, it is crucial to prioritize your safety and well-being throughout your vacation. This book gives crucial recommendations and guidance to guarantee a safe and worry-free time in Rhodes.

1. Research and Plan:

Before your journey, perform a detailed study of the island, including local customs, traditions, and any safety issues. Familiarize yourself with the regions you want to visit, transit alternatives, and emergency contact information. Planning enables you to make educated choices and be better prepared.

2. Stay in Safe Accommodation:

Choose trustworthy and well-reviewed lodgings for your stay in Rhodes. Look for hotels that have security measures in place, such as 24-hour reception, surveillance cameras, and secure access. It is also recommended to keep your room secured and valuables protected in a safe deposit box.

3. Be Aware of Your Surroundings:

Maintain situational awareness everywhere you go. Pay attention to your surroundings, particularly in congested tourist locations, marketplaces, and public transit. Be aware of pickpockets and keep your stuff safe. Avoid flaunting excessive riches or precious objects that may draw unwelcome attention.

4. Use Reliable Transportation:

When going about Rhodes, choose trusted transportation providers. Licensed taxis, licensed bus services, and recognized automobile rental firms are typically safe alternatives. Ensure that cars are in excellent condition, drivers are licensed and agree upon the cost before beginning your trip.

5. Take Precautions on Beaches:

Rhodes is famed for its gorgeous beaches, however, it is necessary to use care when enjoying the sun and water. Swim only in authorized locations with lifeguards on duty. Observe warning indicators and follow any directions offered. Be aware of currents, particularly during windy weather, and avoid swimming alone or in unknown seas.

6. Protect Against the Sun:

Rhodes features a Mediterranean climate, with lots of sunlight throughout the year.

Protect yourself from sunburn and heatstroke by using sunscreen with a high SPF, wearing a hat, sunglasses, and lightweight, breathable clothes. Stay hydrated by drinking lots of water, particularly during the hot summer months.

7. Respect the Local Culture:

Respect for local traditions and cultural norms is vital for a safe and pleasant trip to Rhodes. clothing modestly while visiting religious places and adhering to any special clothing rules. Be nice and courteous to natives, and avoid participating in aggressive or rude conduct.

8. Secure Your Personal Belongings:

Keep your items protected at all times. Carry only essential goods with you and leave unneeded valuables, such as pricey jewelry, at your lodging. Use a money belt or a lockable bag to carry your passport, cash, and other papers. Be careful while using ATMs and conceal your PIN from inquisitive eyes.

9. Stay Connected:

Ensure you have a dependable method of communication throughout your stay in Rhodes. Keep your cell phone charged and have emergency contacts stored. Consider obtaining a local SIM card or enabling international roaming to keep connected with your loved ones and have access to emergency services if required.

10. Trust Your Instincts:

Lastly, trust your intuition. If a situation seems dangerous or unpleasant, remove yourself from it. Avoid secluded regions, particularly at night, and stick to well-lit and busy areas. If you experience any issues or need assistance, seek support from local authorities or call the relevant emergency services.

In Conclusion, By following these safety precautions, you may have a secure and happy time while enjoying the beauties of Rhodes. Remember to be proactive, keep aware of your surroundings, and take appropriate measures. With good preparation, courteous conduct, and awareness, you may completely immerse yourself in the island's beauty, history, and hospitality, knowing that your safety remains a major concern.

The Ideal Rhodes 10 Days itinerary

Rhodes, the picturesque Greek island in the Dodecanese, provides a plethora of activities, from ancient ruins and medieval villages to magnificent beaches and natural marvels. With so much to visit, selecting the right 10-day schedule is vital to make the most of your stay on the island. In this book, we will take you on a detailed trip across Rhodes, emphasizing the must-visit places, historical monuments, cultural activities, and stunning scenery.

Day 1: Arrival in Rhodes Town:

Start your tour by visiting the island's capital, Rhodes Town, a UNESCO World Heritage Site. Begin with a tour around the walled medieval Old Town, meandering through its tiny alleyways, and viewing monuments such as the Palace of the Grand Master and the Street of the Knights. Explore the Archaeological Museum and the Museum of Modern Greek Art to dig into the island's rich history and art culture. End the day by having a sunset supper at a seaside tavern.

Day 2: Lindos:

Travel to the lovely hamlet of Lindos, situated on the east coast of Rhodes. Explore the renowned Acropolis of Lindos, set on a mountaintop and affording panoramic views of the surrounding blue seas. Visit the historic Temple of Athena Lindia and explore the lovely tiny alleyways of the hamlet, filled with whitewashed buildings and traditional architecture. Relax on the gorgeous sandy beaches of Lindos Bay and enjoy great local food at one of the beachfront tavernas.

Day 3: Prasonisi and Windsurfing:

For adventure enthusiasts, drive south to Prasonisi, a tiny piece of land that connects to the main island. Prasonisi is a windsurfer's dream, where the Aegean and Mediterranean waters converge, giving great conditions for windsurfing and kitesurfing. Take lessons or just enjoy watching the experts surf the waves. In the evening, relish a seaside BBQ and revel in the spectacular sunset views.

Day 4: Valley of the Butterflies and Seven Springs:

Embark on a nature-filled day by visiting the Valley of the Butterflies, situated in the western section of Rhodes. Wander through the beautiful valley, where hundreds of butterflies take shelter throughout the summer months. Marvel at the brilliant hues and calm of this unique natural refuge. Afterward, proceed to the Seven Springs, a hidden treasure set in green woodland. Explore the scenic environment, stroll over the wooden bridge, and have a relaxing dip in the crystal-clear waters.

Day 5: Symi Island:

Take a day excursion to the adjacent island of Symi, noted for its colorful neoclassical buildings and gorgeous port. Stroll through the small alleyways of Symi Town, see the Panormitis Monastery, and relax on one of the island's isolated beaches. Enjoy a seafood meal at a seaside taverna and absorb the laidback ambiance of this picturesque island. Return to Rhodes Town in the evening.

Day 6: Ancient Kamiros and Filerimos:

Embark on a historical adventure by visiting the ancient city of Kamiros, situated on the northwest coast of Rhodes. Explore the well-preserved remains of this once-thriving Hellenistic city, including the Agora, the Temple of Athena, and the ancient dwellings. Afterward, travel to Filerimos, a mountain ornamented with a Byzantine monastery and a tall cross. Enjoy magnificent views of the island and discover the relics of the old Acropolis.

Day 7: Tsambika Beach and Monastery:

Spend a day soaking up the sun and enjoying the turquoise waves at Tsambika Beach, situated on the east coast of Rhodes. Relax on the golden sandy beach, swim in the crystal-clear seas, and indulge in beachfront refreshments. Climb the hill to see the Tsambika Monastery, positioned on top, and enjoy beautiful views of the surrounding coastline.

Day 8: Kallithea Springs and Anthony Quinn Bay:

Visit the ancient Kallithea Springs, famed for its medicinal effects and magnificent architecture. Explore the magnificent gardens, ornamented with elaborate mosaics and sculptures, and take a plunge in the soothing thermal waters. Afterward, travel to Anthony Quinn Bay, a lovely cove named after the renowned actor who fell in love with Rhodes during the production of "The Guns of Navarone." Enjoy snorkeling in the crystal-clear seas or just rest on the pebbly beach.

Day 9: Rhodes' West Coast:

Discover the gorgeous west coast of Rhodes by visiting the town of Kamiros Skala, famed for its lovely beach and traditional fishing port. Enjoy delicious seafood at a beach taverna and absorb the laid-back environment. Continue to the lovely town of Embona, located on the slopes of Mount Attavyros. Explore the area's vineyards, taste regional wines, and feel the warm friendliness of the inhabitants.

Day 10: Beach Hopping and Sunset Cruise:

Spend your final day beach hopping along Rhodes' gorgeous coastline. Visit prominent beaches like Faliraki, Tsambika, and Agathi Beach, where you may swim, relax, and enjoy water sports activities. In the evening, go on a sunset cruise, cruising along the coast and experiencing the beautiful hues of the sunset over the Aegean Sea. Toast to an amazing voyage and enjoy a goodbye supper on board.

In Conclusion, With this 10-day itinerary, you will have the chance to discover the varied beauties of Rhodes, from its rich history and cultural legacy to its gorgeous beaches and natural surroundings. Immerse yourself in the island's mesmerizing beauty, delight in great food, and make lasting memories as you discover the pearls of Rhodes. Remember to pace yourself, cherish each moment, and absorb the beauty that greets you on this amazing Greek island.

RHODES CULTURAL CUSTOMS

Rhodes, the enchanting Greek island in the Dodecanese, has a rich cultural legacy that spans millennia. The island's customs and traditions are firmly ingrained in its history and impacted by numerous civilizations. In this book, we will examine the cultural customs of Rhodes, shining light on the island's distinctive traditions, social etiquette, and vivid events that characterize the local way of life.

1. Hospitality and Filoxenia:

Hospitality, or philoxenia, is at the foundation of Rhodes' cultural fabric. The inhabitants of Rhodes are noted for their friendly and inviting demeanor, making tourists feel at home. When visiting someone's house or a local company, expect to be treated with real hospitality and charity. It is usual to return this compassion by showing thanks and observing local norms.

2. Religious Celebrations and Customs:

Religion plays a vital part in the life of Rhodians, with Greek Orthodox Christianity being the main religion. Religious holidays and rituals are followed throughout the year. Easter carries great importance, with somber processions, religious services, and the midnight Resurrection Mass. It is typical to share the traditional greeting "Christos Anesti" (Christ has risen) around this period.

3. Traditional Cuisine:

Rhodes enjoys a diverse culinary legacy that reflects its cultural norms. Traditional recipes generally use local ingredients, such as olive oil, fresh vegetables, herbs, and fish. Mezedes, a variety of tiny meals, are a typical component of Greek cuisine. Sharing meals and participating in spirited discussions around the table is important to the Rhodian eating experience.

4. Folklore and Traditional Music:

Rhodes has a lively folkloric history that is exhibited via song, dance, and costumes. The island's traditional music, known as "paleo," is characterized by energetic rhythms and instruments like the lyre and violin. Traditional dances, such as the "shirts" and "kalamatas," are commonly performed at weddings, festivals, and cultural events, allowing residents and guests to engage in the festivities.

5. Wedding Traditions:

Weddings are major occasions in Rhodes, celebrated with tremendous excitement and respect for age-old traditions. Traditional Rhodian marriages involve elaborate rituals, where the bride is decked in white attire with a crimson veil representing good luck. Guests sprinkle the newlyweds with rice and flower petals as a sign of fertility and blessings. Festive music, dancing, and scrumptious feasts are major parts of these festive events.

6. Respect for Monuments and Archaeological Sites:

Rhodes is home to a multitude of historical monuments and archaeological sites, including the ancient city of Rhodes and the medieval Old Town. Respecting and protecting these cultural assets is crucial. Visitors should keep to specified walkways, abstain from touching or destroying buildings, and obey any directions presented. By exhibiting respect for the island's past, we can assure its preservation for future generations.

7. Carnival Celebrations:

Carnival, or "Apokries," is a colorful and joyous season in Rhodes, observed in the weeks coming up to Lent. The island comes alive with colorful parades, masquerade parties, and street festivals. Locals dress in extravagant costumes, and traditional masks and dance performances add to the carnival mood. It is a time for fun, pleasure, and embracing the lighthearted side of Rhodes' cultural customs.

8. Traditional Handicrafts:

Rhodes is noted for its long legacy of craftsmanship, with artists adept in different ancient skills. The island is famed for delicate lacework called "panel," handcrafted pottery, woodcarving, and woven fabrics. Visitors have the chance to observe these crafts being done directly in workshops and marketplaces, and buying these unique mementos promotes the preservation of these traditional arts.

9. Respect for Elders and Family Values:

Respect for elders and strong family relationships are profoundly engrained in Rhodes' cultural practices. It is common to welcome elderly folks with a warm handshake or a kiss on the cheek, as a symbol of respect. Family gatherings and dinners are treasured times when various generations get together to share tales, knowledge, and love.

10. Annual Cultural Festivals:

Throughout the year, Rhodes offers different cultural events that display its creative legacy. The Medieval Rose Festival, hosted in the picturesque Old Town, takes visitors back in time with reenactments, music, and dramatic performances. The Rhodes International Festival comprises famous performers from Greece and beyond, offering concerts, musicals, and dance acts. These events serve as a platform to highlight and promote Rhodes' cultural variety.

In Conclusion, Rhodes' cultural practices are a monument to the island's rich history and the continuing vitality of its people. By adopting these customs, tourists may immerse themselves in the native way of life and get a greater understanding of the island's cultural legacy. Whether engaging in joyous events, eating local food, or seeing traditional arts, experiencing Rhodes' cultural practices is a voyage of discovery and connection to the island's dynamic history and present.

10 Best Hotels In Rhodes

Rhodes, the lovely Greek island in the Dodecanese, provides a selection of great hotels that appeal to varied interests and budgets. From luxury beachside resorts to quaint boutique hotels, Rhodes offers something to meet every traveler's requirements. In this guide, we will dig into the top hotels in Rhodes, showcasing their distinct features, services, and locations to help you make an educated selection for your stay on this enchanting island.

1. Atrium Platinum Luxury Resort Hotel & Spa:

Located in Ixia, only a short distance from Rhodes Town, the Atrium Platinum Luxury Resort Hotel & Spa provides an amazing combination of elegance, luxury, and spectacular sea views. This 5-star hotel has big rooms and suites, a private beach, numerous swimming pools, a spa, and outstanding dining choices. Immerse yourself in luxury and luxuriate in the hotel's world-class amenities and outstanding service.

2. Lindos Blu Luxury Hotel & Suites:

Perched on a cliff overlooking the Aegean Sea, the Lindos Blu Luxury Hotel & Suites in Vlycha Bay is a refuge of tranquillity and luxury. With its modern architecture, infinity pools, and breathtaking sea views, this adults-only hotel emanates an environment of sheer tranquility. The hotel's large rooms and suites, gourmet restaurants, and spa facilities provide a wonderful and refreshing visit.

3. Mitsis Grand Hotel:

Located in the center of Rhodes Town, the Mitsis Grand Hotel blends historical elegance with contemporary luxury. This 5-star hotel provides exquisite accommodations, a rooftop swimming pool with panoramic views, and direct access to a private beach. With its central position, visitors can easily explore the city's attractions, including the UNESCO-listed Old Town, museums, and busy markets.

4. Sheraton Rhodes Resort:

Nestled on the magnificent Ixia Bay, the Sheraton Rhodes Resort provides a sumptuous hideaway with its opulent accommodations, lagoon-style swimming pools, and direct beach access. This family-friendly resort features a broad selection of services, including kids' clubs, various restaurants, a spa, and sports facilities. Enjoy spectacular sunsets over the Aegean Sea while enjoying the famous Sheraton hospitality.

5. Rodos Palace Hotel:

Set within beautiful gardens overlooking the sea, the Rodos Palace Hotel is a famous 5-star hotel located on the outskirts of Rhodes Town. With its large accommodations, comprehensive recreational facilities, and private beach, this hotel appeals to both families and couples seeking a premium break. The Rodos Palace includes three swimming pools, tennis courts, a spa, and a choice of eating options.

6. Atrium Prestige Thalasso Spa Resort & Villas:

Situated in the calm town of Lachania on the southeastern coast of Rhodes, the Atrium Prestige Thalasso Spa Resort & Villas provides a serene getaway in a lovely location. This 5-star resort has exquisite accommodations, private villas with pools, a luxury spa, and direct access to a Blue Flag beach. Indulge in the resort's thalassotherapy treatments and enjoy the tranquil environment of this exquisite setting.

7. D'Andrea Mare Beach Hotel:

Located in the popular resort town of Ialyssos, the D'Andrea Mare Beach Hotel provides a blend of comfort, affordability, and an excellent beachfront position. This family-friendly hotel provides contemporary accommodations, a spacious swimming pool, a kids' club, and close access to the beach. With its accessible location and variety of services, it is a fantastic option for families seeking a wonderful beach holiday.

8. Boutique 5 Hotel & Spa:

Nestled in the town of Kiotari on the southeastern coast of Rhodes, the Boutique 5 Hotel & Spa provides a magnificent and exclusive getaway for adults only. This boutique hotel has contemporary accommodations, a tranquil spa, numerous swimming pools, and direct access to a private beach. Enjoy the customized attention and calm ambiance that make this hotel a truly hidden treasure.

9. Eden Roc Resort Hotel:

Situated on the gorgeous Kalithea Bay, the Eden Roc Resort Hotel blends spectacular natural beauty with modern comforts. This family-friendly resort provides comfortable accommodations, a huge swimming pool complex, a water park, and direct beach access. The hotel's active entertainment program and numerous food choices provide a fun-filled and memorable stay for visitors of all ages.

10. AquaGrand Exclusive Deluxe Resort:

Located in the picturesque hamlet of Lindos, the AquaGrand Exclusive Deluxe Resort is an adult-only getaway with magnificent accommodations, an infinity pool overlooking the sea, and direct beach access. With its minimalist design, luxury facilities, and dedicated service, this resort offers a calm and romantic vacation for couples seeking seclusion and relaxation.

In Conclusion, Rhodes provides a wonderful assortment of hotels that cater to varied desires, from opulent resorts with vast amenities to boutique hideaways with customized care. Whether you prefer extravagance, family-friendly facilities, or a romantic hideaway, the top hotels in Rhodes provide a blend of comfort, gorgeous views, and accessible locations to enhance your stay on this enchanting island. Choose the hotel that matches your tastes, and be ready for an amazing vacation surrounded by the beauty of Rhodes.

Top 10 Beaches In Rhodes

Rhodes, the biggest of the Dodecanese islands in Greece, is famed for its stunning beaches that provide pure seas, golden sands, and magnificent coastline vistas. In this guide, we will examine the greatest beaches in Rhodes, emphasizing their distinct characteristics, activities, and facilities to help you plan an enjoyable beach holiday.

1. Faliraki Beach:

Located on the northeastern coast of Rhodes, Faliraki Beach is one of the island's most popular and colorful beaches. Its lengthy stretch of fine sand and crystal-clear seas make it great for sunbathing and swimming. Faliraki Beach provides several activities, including beach bars, watersports facilities, and sunbed rentals. In the nights, the beach changes into a bustling area with beach parties and entertainment alternatives.

2. Lindos Beach:

Situated on the southeastern coast of Rhodes in the lovely hamlet of Lindos, Lindos Beach is noted for its picturesque location and magnificent vistas. The beach is encircled by stunning cliffs and viewed by the majestic Acropolis of Lindos. The crystal-clear blue seas and golden beaches create a quiet and pleasant ambiance. Visitors may enjoy sunbathing, swimming, and touring the picturesque hamlet of Lindos nearby.

3. Tsambika Beach:

Located on the eastern coast of Rhodes, Tsambika Beach is a hidden treasure that provides a pure and untouched natural environment. With its golden sand and shallow, quiet seas, it's a perfect beach for families with children. The beach is bordered by cliffs, giving a picturesque background. Climb up to the Tsambika Monastery, built on a neighboring hill, offering panoramic views of the beach and surrounding scenery.

4. Anthony Quinn Bay:

Nestled between Faliraki and Ladiko, Anthony Quinn Bay is a tiny, lovely beach named after the renowned actor who fell in love with its beauty while shooting "The Guns of Navarone." This quiet cove is highlighted by its emerald-green seas, rugged cliffs, and lush flora. Snorkeling fans will be amazed by the underwater environment filled with marine life. The beach provides sunbed rentals and a modest seaside tavern.

5. Prasonisi Beach:

For anyone seeking a unique beach experience, Prasonisi Beach on the southernmost part of Rhodes is a must-visit. What makes this beach special is its geological formation—a sandbar that links the main island to a tiny islet at low tide. Prasonisi is a sanctuary for windsurfers and kitesurfers because of the high winds and ideal circumstances. Even if you're not into water sports, witnessing the multicolored sails against the background of the Aegean Sea is a sight to behold.

6. Kallithea Beach:

Situated next to the famed Kallithea Springs, Kallithea Beach is noted for its picturesque surroundings and good amenities. The beach has loungers, umbrellas, and crystal-clear seas suitable for swimming and snorkeling. The neighboring Kallithea Springs provide a touch of history and elegance to the region, making it a distinctive beach destination.

7. Agathi Beach:

Tucked away on the eastern coast of Rhodes, Agathi Beach is a serene and unspoiled refuge with beautiful white sand and calm blue waves. Surrounded by rocky hills and abundant foliage, it provides a calm getaway away from the crowded tourist regions. Facilities are modest, enabling guests to appreciate the natural beauty of the beach undisturbed.

8. Pefkos Beach:

Located in the resort village of Pefkos, Pefkos Beach is a favorite among tourists seeking a quiet and family-friendly ambiance. The beach provides a combination of soft sand and pebbles, with shallow waves excellent for swimming and paddling. Pefkos Beach is well-equipped with loungers, parasols, and water sports equipment. The surrounding town provides a choice of restaurants, stores, and lodgings.

9. Agios Pavlos Beach:

Tucked away on the southern coast of Rhodes, Agios Pavlos Beach provides a private and serene location. Surrounded by cliffs and accessible through a winding road, this hidden treasure is great for anyone seeking seclusion and natural beauty. The beach has smooth sand, clean waves, and a quiet ambiance. Keep in mind that facilities are limited, so come prepared with supplies.

10. Ixia Beach:

Situated on the northwestern coast of Rhodes, Ixia Beach provides a unique combination of natural beauty and contemporary conveniences. The beach is famed for its high winds, making it popular among windsurfers and kitesurfers.

Sunbeds, umbrellas, and water sports equipment rentals are easily available. Ixia Beach is also conveniently adjacent to Rhodes Town, allowing easy access to shopping, eating, and entertainment opportunities.

In Conclusion, Rhodes has a broad assortment of beaches, each with its special charm and attractions. Whether you're seeking exciting beach parties, calm isolation, water sports experiences, or family-friendly environs, the greatest beaches in Rhodes appeal to a variety of interests. Explore these gorgeous coastal treasures, soak up the sun, and immerse yourself in the splendor of the Aegean Sea for an amazing beach experience in Rhodes.

Do's and Don'ts' In Rhodes

When visiting Rhodes, it's necessary to be aware of the local traditions and etiquette to guarantee a nice and courteous experience. Here are some do's and don'ts to keep in mind throughout your stay:

Do's:

1. Respect local norms and traditions:

Greece, particularly Rhodes, has a rich cultural past. Respect local norms, such as covering your shoulders and knees while visiting holy places and removing your shoes before entering someone's house.

2. Try Greek cuisine:

Rhodes provides a superb choice of classic Greek meals. Do indulge in the local food, explore new tastes, and appreciate the excellent Greek dishes.

3. Explore the historical sites:

Rhodes is rich in history, with amazing ancient remains and medieval buildings. Do take the time to explore historical places like the Rhodes Old Town, the Acropolis of Rhodes, and the Palace of the Grand Master to immerse yourself in the island's intriguing history.

4. Enjoy the beaches responsibly:

Rhodes is famed for its stunning beaches. Do enjoy the sun, beach, and water, but remember to obey any safety recommendations and respect the environment by not leaving garbage behind.

5. Interact with the locals:

Greeks are famed for their great friendliness. Do participate in polite talks with the locals, ask for advice, and embrace the chance to learn more about their culture and way of life.

Don'ts:

1. Don't litter:

Keep Rhodes clean and maintain its natural beauty by disposing of your rubbish appropriately. Use specified garbage containers and recycling facilities to preserve the cleanliness of the island.

2. Don't touch old objects or ruins:

Rhodes is home to historical treasures. Do not touch or remove any items or harm the ruins while visiting archaeological sites. It's crucial to conserve these cultural riches for future generations.

3. Avoid excessive public demonstrations of affection:

While Greeks are typically friendly and loving, it's important to avoid excessive public shows of love, since it may be deemed improper in some contexts.

4. Don't haggle excessively:

Bargaining is a widespread activity in various marketplaces and stores in Rhodes. However, don't press too hard or haggle excessively, since it may be considered as impolite. Use your discretion and negotiate nicely and pleasantly.

5. Avoid unsuitable clothing:

Rhodes is a tourist attraction, but it's still vital to dress correctly, particularly when visiting religious sites or more conservative places. Avoid too exposing apparel and opt for a modest dress to show respect for local norms.

By following these do's and don'ts, you may assure a courteous and pleasurable experience throughout your vacation to Rhodes. Embrace the local culture, soak in the history, and make lasting experiences on this beautiful island.

Most Frequently Ask Questions (FAQ) About Rhodes

Rhodes, commonly known as the Island of the Knights, is one of the most popular tourist attractions in Greece. With its rich history, magnificent beaches, and dynamic culture, Rhodes draws travelers from all over the globe. If you're considering a vacation to Rhodes, you may have numerous questions in mind. In this guide, we will answer the most commonly asked questions regarding Rhodes and give extensive explanations for each subject.

1. Where is Rhodes located?

Rhodes is situated in the southeastern Aegean Sea, off the coast of Turkey. It is the biggest island in the Dodecanese archipelago and sits roughly 11 miles (18 kilometers) southwest of the Turkish mainland.

2. How can I go to Rhodes?

Rhodes has an international airport, Diagoras International Airport, which services both local and international flights. Many major airlines provide direct flights to Rhodes from different European locations. Alternatively, you may also reach Rhodes by ferry from Piraeus, the major port of Athens, or other surrounding Greek islands.

3. What is the ideal time to visit Rhodes?

The optimum time to visit Rhodes is during the spring (April to June) and fall (September to October) seasons. During these months, the weather is nice, with warm temperatures and fewer people compared to the busy summer months. However, if you prefer warmer weather for swimming and beach activities, the summer months of July and August are equally popular.

4. What are the must-visit attractions in Rhodes?

Rhodes provides a wealth of sites to visit. Some of the must-visit attractions are the UNESCO World Heritage-listed Rhodes Old Town, the Palace of the Grand Master, the Acropolis of Rhodes, the Ancient Kamiros, the Valley of the Butterflies, and the gorgeous beaches of Lindos and Faliraki.

5. Is it required to hire a vehicle in Rhodes?

Renting a vehicle in Rhodes is not compulsory but might be advantageous, particularly if you want to explore the island at your leisure. Public transportation alternatives, including buses and taxis, are available and can take you to most main tourist locations. However, owning a vehicle provides you with more freedom and enables you to explore off-the-beaten-path destinations.

6. What are the notable beaches in Rhodes?

Rhodes features various lovely beaches. Some of the renowned ones are Tsambika Beach, Faliraki Beach, Anthony Quinn Bay, Lindos Beach, and Elli Beach. Each beach has its distinct appeal, from crystal-clear waves to golden sand and water sports activities.

7. Are there any water sports activities in Rhodes?

Yes, Rhodes is heaven for water sports fans. You may enjoy activities like snorkeling, scuba diving, windsurfing, jet skiing, and parasailing at numerous beaches and water sports facilities throughout the island.

Whether you're a novice or an experienced explorer, there's something for everyone.

8. What typical meals should I try in Rhodes?

Rhodes has a rich culinary past, and there are various classic dishes worth sampling. Some popular examples are "parousia" (chickpea fritters), "lachanodolmades" (stuffed cabbage rolls), "souvlaki" (grilled meat skewers), "tzatziki" (yogurt and cucumber dip), and "loukoumades" (honey-soaked dough balls).

9. Can I visit other Greek islands from Rhodes?

Yes, Rhodes is an ideal location for island hopping in the Dodecanese archipelago. You may easily explore surrounding islands such as Symi, Kos, Kalymnos, and Patmos. Regular ferry services run between these islands, enabling you to explore more of the Greek island paradise.

10. Is it safe to go to Rhodes?

Rhodes is usually regarded as a safe place for vacationers. However, it's always vital to take conventional safety measures, such as being alert to your surroundings, keeping a check on your stuff, and following any local standards or instructions. As with any trip location, it's important to carry travel insurance for peace of mind.

In conclusion, Rhodes provides a lovely combination of history, culture, and natural beauty, making it a sought-after holiday site. By answering these commonly asked questions, we aim to have given you a full overview of Rhodes and its attractions. Plan your vacation thoughtfully, and spend your time touring this wonderful island!

Conclusion

As your stay on Rhodes comes to a close, we hope that our travel guide has given you the tools and insights to make the most of your visit to this lovely island. Rhodes has left an unforgettable stamp on your heart, as its rich history, magnificent vistas, and kind hospitality have created a tapestry of memories that will remain with you long after you go.

From roaming the old alleys of Rhodes Town and marveling at the vestiges of its medieval history to discovering the calm towns and picturesque beaches that dot the coastline, you have experienced the spirit of Rhodes in all its beauty. Perhaps you have dived into the island's thriving culinary scene, delighting in traditional specialties and enjoying local wines, or engaged in adrenaline excursions, such as scuba diving in the crystal-clear seas or trekking through the rocky interior.

Yet, Rhodes is a site that invites repeat visits. The island's charm is eternal, and there will always be more to find, more tales to unravel, and more moments to appreciate. Whether you prefer to dig further into its history, delve into the natural beauty of its neighboring islands, or just immerse yourself in the island's laid-back rhythm, Rhodes will welcome you with open arms.

As you wave goodbye to this enchanting island, take with you the warmth of its people, the echoes of its tales, and the grandeur of its scenery. Let the spirit of Rhodes inspire you to embrace new experiences, seek hidden jewels, and approach the world with a revitalized sense of curiosity.

Thank you for allowing us to be your guide on this trip. May your memories of Rhodes stay vivid, and may they fuel the flame of wanderlust inside you for years to come. Farewell, lovely traveler, until we meet again on the beaches of Rhodes.

Made in United States
North Haven, CT
21 June 2023